Handbook for the Confraternity of the Most Holy Rosary

– Revised Edition –

Michail P. Ford, O.P.

Office of the Promoter of Confraternity of the Holy Rosary, Central Province Dominicans, USA.

NEW PRIORY PRESS

EXPLORING THE DOMINICAN VISION

Cover Artist: Susan Webb
Production Editor: Albert Judy, O.P.
Copyright © 2014 Dominican Province of St. Albert the Great (U.S.A.).
All rights reserved. Published by New Priory Press,
1910 South Ashland Avenue, Chicago, IL 60608
www.NewPrioryPress.com

TABLE OF CONTENTS

INTRODUCTION: WHAT IS THE CONFRATERNITY OF THE HOLY ROSARY? vii

PART I   LEGISLATION FOR ROSARY SOCIETIES 1

1 The Purpose of the Rosary Society 1
2 Obligations of Membership 1
3 Admission of Members 3
    Conditions of Membership 3
    Manner of Admission 4
    Who May Receive Members? 5
4 The Privileges and Benefits of the Rosary Confraternity . 6
5 The Chapel or Altar of the Rosary Confraternity 7
6 The Administration of the Rosary Confraternity 8
    The Master of the Dominican Order
    and the Local Prior Provincial 8
    The Provincial Director or Promoter of the Rosary
      Confraternity 9
    The Local Director of the Confraternity 9
    Appointment of the Local Director. 10
    The Duties of the Local Director. 11
    Special Organization of the Confraternity 12
7 The Establishment of the Confraternity 13
    The Place of Establishment 13
    Petition for the Establishment 14
    The Transferal of the Confraternity 14
    In Cases of Doubtful 15

   8 Sample By-Laws of the Rosary Altar Society 16

PART II ROSARIAN RITUAL AND FORMULARY 21

   1 Manner of Establishing the Confraternity
of the Holy Rosary 21

   2 Solemn Reception Ceremony for Rosary Society
Members 23

   3 Installation of Officers 25

**PART III ROSARY FORMULARY AND BLESSINGS FOR
DIRECTORS OF SOCIETIES OF THE ROSARY 27**

   1 Blessing of Rosaries 27

      Short Formula for Blessing of Rosaries 28

   2 Blessing of Roses 28

   3 Blessing of Candles 29

   4 Blessing of Rosary Medals or Pins 29

PART IV ROSARIAN CUSTOMS AND DEVOTIONS 31

   1 The Monthly Rosary Procession 31

   2 Rosary Candles and Roses 32

   3 The Fifteen Saturdays of the Rosary 33

   4 Rosary for the Dead 33

   5 The Family Rosary 34

   6 Promises of Our Lady, Queen of the Rosary
Given to Blessed Alan De Rupe, O.P.
– Founder of the Confraternity 35

   7 Rosary Novenas 36

      Order of Exercises of the Rosary Novena 37

   8 The Dominican Way of Praying the Rosary 39

      The Joyful Mysteries 40

      The Sorrowful Mysteries 40

      The Luminous Mysteries 41

  The Glorious Mysteries 41
  Concluding Prayers of the Five Decades. 41
9 Optional Rosary Prayers 42
  Prayer After the Joyful Mysteries 42
  Prayer After the Sorrowful Mysteries......................... 43
  Prayer After the Luminous Mysteries 43
  Prayer After the Glorious Mysteries 43
10 Prayer for the Rosary Apostolate of the Confraternity . 44
11 Rules on Indulgences.. 44
12 Indulgences Granted to the Members
  of the Rosary Confraternity 46
APPENDIX: CONTACTS **47**

INTRODUCTION: WHAT IS THE CONFRATERNITY OF THE HOLY ROSARY?

> "The Dominican Order, which from its very beginning has been most devoted in honoring the Blessed Virgin, and by which the institution and propagation of the Confraternity of the Rosary was accomplished, holds as its inheritance all that belongs to this devotion."
>
> – Pope Leo XIII, *Ubi Primum*, n. 1.

The Confraternity of the Most Holy Rosary has existed for over half a millennium. It began in the 1470s through Blessed Alan de la Roche, O.P.'s preaching and devotion to Our Blessed Mother. It quickly spread through the world. Over the centuries, countless Catholics have grown in their relationship Christ and His Church with help of Our Blessed Mother and her Rosary under the direction of the Dominican Friars, or the Order of Friars Preachers as we are also known.

The simplicity of the confraternity, also known as the Rosary Society or the Rosary Altar Society in the United States, has also added to its success. The only obligation it asks of its members is to pray the Rosary once a week and does not bind this promise by pain of sin. The benefits to its members are substantial. Apart from the spiritual growth one receives from praying the Rosary regularly, confraternity members also grow in their sense of community. The prayers and good works of the entire confraternity are added to all of the prayers and works of the Dominican Order (and in both cases for members both living and deceased). In essence the Confraternity of the Most Holy Rosary is the largest spiritual bouquet the world has ever known. There are also numerous opportunities for members to gain partial and plenary indulgences.

With the renewal of traditional Catholic devotional practices on the rise, and at the request of the Master of the Dominican Order, the Dominican promoters of the confraternity in the United States have been meeting with the goal of finding new ways to introduce the faithful to this wonderful Dominican prayer ministry. The updating of the Rosarian's Handbook is the first fruits of these meetings.

Much of what is contained here comes (with permission) from the *Revised Third Edition of the Rosarian's Handbook* published by our brother friars in Dominican Province of St. Joseph in the Eastern United States. Because the rules establishing the confraternity—last revised by Pope Leo XIII in 1898 in the Apostolic Constitution *Ubi Primum*—have only been amended once in 1980, there was very little in the nuts and bolts of how the confraternity is governed which needed updating. Many thanks go out to those brothers in the past who originally wrote and edited the material.

Catholic faithful may enroll in the Confraternity through any of the Dominican Provinces by contacting their local Provincial Promoter of the Holy Rosary.

Michail P. Ford, O.P.
Promoter of the Confraternity of the Holy Rosary
Dominican Province of St. Albert the Great
OPCentral.org

PART I

LEGISLATION FOR ROSARY SOCIETIES

These regulations are based on the Constitution *Ubi Primum* of Pope Leo the VIII.

1 The Purpose of the Rosary Society

The primary purpose of the Confraternity of the Holy Rosary or the Society of the Rosary Altar or Rosary Society is "to praise and honor the Blessed Virgin Mary and to secure her patronage by the recitation of the Rosary for the mutual spiritual benefit of all the members throughout the world."

2 Obligations of Membership

"The only obligation of the members of the Confraternity…is to recite the fifteen mysteries of the Rosary…once a week."

The conditions of this obligation are:
- It does not bind under pain of sin.
- Meditation on the mysteries is necessary.
- "In meditating on the mysteries of Our Redemption, other mysteries should not be substituted for those in general use. The Apostolic See has already decreed that those who do not observe the usual order in meditating on the mysteries do not gain the indulgence of the Rosary."
- The true form of the Rosary must be used, so that it should always be composed of either five, ten, or fifteen decades.
- All members of the Confraternity are to be included in the intentions each member's Rosary. A general intention suffices and it need not be renewed each time.

- The fifteen decades need not be said at one time, but may be divided into decades and recited when convenient, as long as the fifteen decades are said during the week.
- This obligation does not imply the recitation of an extra fifteen decades if one recites the Rosary frequently, for example if one is accustomed to recite five decades a day.

In 2002 St. John Paul II added the luminous mysteries to the Rosary in his apostolic letter *Rosarium Virginis Mariae*. Since then it has become normative to include the luminous mysteries and highly recommended for Confraternities of the Holy Rosary. However, at this time the original fifteen mysteries fifteen are all that are required to gain the indulgences granted to the Confraternity.

Other Traditional Exercises of Members of the Rosary Society

The following are recommended exercises and are not the primary obligation of Rosarians. Membership only requires the recitation of the full Rosary each week under the conditions given above. However, in order to foster greater devotion to the Rosary and unity within the Confraternity, these traditional observances can very helpful.

- Corporate reception of Holy Communion on a specified day each month as a Confraternity or group.
- Attendance at the regularly scheduled Confraternity meetings if applicable.
- Assisting the parish by leading the public recitation of the Rosary. If your parish has a Rosary Altar it is preferred, although not necessary, that it take place at the Rosary Altar. A Rosary Altar is not a requirement of the Confraternity. Some churches were built the traditional

Rosary Altars that depicts the Blessed Virgin giving the Rosary to St. Dominic.
- Establishment of and assistance at a monthly Rosary Procession.

3 Admission of Members

Conditions of Membership

These conditions are not specific for the Rosary Society, but are general conditions laid down in Canon Law for membership in any Confraternity. Knowledge of these conditions is necessary since persons ineligible are quite often proposed for membership.

- Any living Catholic who has the use of reason may be admitted.
- A candidate must know of and consent to her or his enrollment and be willing to fulfill the obligations of the Society.
- A candidate need not be physically present to be enrolled, but there must be evidence of his or her wish to be a member.
- The deceased may not be enrolled as members.
- Membership in the Confraternity of the Holy Rosary does not prohibit membership in other Confraternities, Pious Unions and Societies.
- No fee may be charged for admission itself. A donation may be asked for incidental expenses (postage, books, etc.).
- And lastly, the fulfillment of the requirement for admission as given below.

Manner of Admission

To share in the spiritual benefits and privileges of the Rosary Confraternity, the names of members of the Rosary Society should be inscribed in the Official Register of a Church where the Rosary Confraternity has been canonically established. This enrollment is essential for membership.

There two methods of admission:
- Simple Form. This is the inscription of the name in the Register, as stated above. This may be done any day.
- Solemn Form. In addition to the mere inscription of the names, there is a solemn ceremony to mark the entrance into the Confraternity. The form of the ceremony can be found in Part II of this handbook, Rosarian Ritual and Formulary.

The following points are to be noted in regard to admission:

> The Rosary Confraternity must be canonically established and an Official Register must be kept, otherwise it does not enjoy the spiritual benefits granted to it. "Whatever solidarity may be hereafter established cannot enjoy any of the benefits, privileges and indulgences with which the Roman Pontiffs have enriched the lawful character and true Confraternity of the Rosary unless a Charter of Institution be obtained from the Dominican Order." (Applications for this Charter should be sent to the Promoter of the Confraternity of the Holy Rosary, 1910 S. Ashland Ave., Chicago, IL 60608. Rosary@opcentral.org)

The burden of inscription is upon the priest who receives the names. New members begin to participate in the benefits of the Confraternity at the moment they signify their intention to a priest who has the necessary faculties, and also the responsibility to have them inscribed.

If the inscription of the names in the Official Register of a Local or Provincial Confraternity is delayed or neglected, the members are nevertheless in full possession of their rights and privileges as members.

The Director does not need to inscribe personally the names in the Register. The names may be written in by another priest or a lay person, but the Director must approve and sign the bottom of each page.

Since all Local Confraternities have full rights and privileges, membership is valid throughout the world. Hence, if a member moves, there is no need to reenter the new Confraternity. One reception is sufficient. A means of identification for a new Local Confraternity is all that is needed.

Who May Receive Members?

The faculty to receive members into the Confraternity is limited, that is, not every priest may do it, but only those who have faculties. The following have faculties:

- Dominican priests who have faculties for hearing confession in the Order.
- Provincial and Local Directors of the Confraternity. Their faculties are according to the limitations stated in the document of their appointment.
- Priests who have received special faculties from the Master of the Dominican Order, the local Prior Provincial, or the Holy See. These faculties are granted according to the terms of their concession and they should be carefully examined to determine their exact extent. To obtain these faculties, diocesan priests should apply through their Chancery Offices and Religious through their Major Superiors.

4 The Privileges and Benefits of the Rosary Confraternity

The Privileges and Benefits to which members of the Confraternity are entitled are of two kinds: Intrinsic and Extrinsic.

The Intrinsic Benefits are the Indulgences which have been granted to members of the Confraternity. A complete list of these indulgences is found at the end of this book.

The Extrinsic Benefits come under two headings:

First, the participation in life, at death and after death in all the prayers and good works of all the members of the Confraternity.
It "binds them to one another by no other bond than the recitation of the Rosary of Mary. The result is that, while each one contributes a little toward the common treasure, all receive a great deal from it. For whenever members fulfill their obligation of reciting the Rosary according to the rule of the Confraternity, they include in their intentions all its members, and they in turn render them the same service multiplied." This is a special privilege of the Rosary Confraternity. Considering the thousands upon thousands of members who weekly recite the Rosary, the participation in all those prayers alone is a very consoling and powerful bond of spiritual communion. To have the constant power of all this spiritual force to help in our daily lives, to give courage at the hour of death, and to liberate us from purgatory after death, is a great privilege.

Second, is the participation in the good works of the Dominican Order. This participation means that all the good works—prayers, mortifications, apostolic works for the salvation of souls, Masses, suffrages—of the whole Order, throughout the world (past, present and future) are shared with the members of the Rosary Confraternity, which the Order considers as a part of the Dominican Family.

5 The Chapel or Altar of the Rosary Confraternity

The Document of Establishment of the Rosary Confraternity speaks of a Chapel or Altar of the Confraternity. The necessary information in this regard is contained in the following statements:

- If possible (and in most churches it is not, since it requires special planning), there may be a chapel reserved to the Rosary Confraternity. Where this is possible it is very convenient, since there the Confraternity may hold its functions, indulgences may be gained, etc.
- Where a chapel is not possible, a side altar or the main altar of the church is to be used.
- Many Confraternities may use the same altar, so that the altar does not have to be given exclusively to the Rosary Confraternity.
- This altar should be designated at the time the Confraternity is established, by the priest officiating and should be noted in the Instrument of Establishment.
- The altar should have some mark that it is the Confraternity Altar. The Document of Establishment states that it should be a statue or picture of St. Dominic receiving the Rosary from the Blessed Virgin Mary on or near the altar. The installation of the statue or picture does not have to be done at once. Also because of particular circumstances it may prove impossible. In any case some kind of marker should be attached to the altar.

6 The Administration of the Rosary Confraternity

The Administration of the Rosary Confraternity is quite clearly laid out according to Canon Law, the acts of the Sovereign Pontiffs, decrees and decisions of the Holy See, the Constitutions of the Dominican Order, and the regulations of the Dominican Order. The material can be divided into the three following sections:

The Master of the Dominican Order and the Local Prior Provincial

The Master of the Order is the supreme Moderator of the Rosary Confraternity. "The Dominican Order, which from its very beginning has been most devoted in honoring the Blessed Virgin, and by which the institution and propagation of the Confraternity of the Rosary was accomplished, holds as its inheritance all that belongs to this devotion." This commission from the Holy See in regard to the Rosary Confraternity is exercised by the Master of the Order and the Local Prior Provincial. Since 1980, at the request of the Master of the Order and the General Chapter of Quezon City (1977), the Pontifical Council for the Laity granted a rescript to the Order so that Rosary Confraternities could be erected in parishes directly by the local Prior Provincial.

The following powers belong to the Master of the Order and Prior Provincial:

> "Only the Master of the Dominicans, therefore, is to have the right of establishing sodalities of the Rosary. When he is absent from Rome, his Vicar General has the right; and when he dies or is removed from his office, it belongs to the Vicar General of the Order."
> "For the establishment of the Confraternity in any particular church, the Master of the Order is to depute by the

usual document, a priest of his own Order; where there are no convents of Dominican Fathers, he is to appoint a priest approved of by the Bishop."

The Provincial Director or Promoter of the Rosary Confraternity

The administration of the Confraternity for practical purposes is broken down to smaller units. In each Province of the Dominican Order, a worldwide organization, there is a Provincial Director of the Confraternity. Sometimes he is referred to as the Provincial Promoter of the Confraternity. This appointment is made by the Province itself. The principal function of his office is to promote the Confraternity within the limits of the Province and to act as the representative for the Master of the Order and to handle all necessary business for the Confraternity in reference to the Master of the Order through his Provincial.

All matters concerning the Confraternity and in fact the Rosary may and should be referred to the proper Provincial Director. For convenience, the following is the Headquarters of the Provincial Director of the Rosary Confraternity:

Promoter of Confraternity of the Holy Rosary
1910 S. Ashland Ave.
Chicago, IL 60608
Rosary@opcentral.org

The Local Director of the Confraternity

The last unit in the administration of the Confraternity is the Local Confraternity itself. This is the Confraternity established in a parish church or a religious church or chapel. All the rest of the regulations and details of administration are designed and intended for this unit, which is the most important in the whole picture, since it is the local unit which actually carries out the work of the Confraternity. The whole notion of the Confraternity functions in this, its fundamental unit.

Each Local Confraternity is complete in itself, enjoys all the rights and privileges of the Confraternity and is equal to any other unit of the Confraternity. "Since there is no Archconfraternity of the Most Holy Rosary to which the lesser sodalities are aggregated, it follows that each new association of the Rosary, by its own canonical institution, enjoys all the indulgences and privileges which are granted by the Apostolic See to the other sodalities of the Rosary throughout the world."

The moderator of the Local Confraternity is the Local Director. Since he presides over the fundamental unit of the Confraternity, his office is most important for the welfare of the Confraternity. In large measure the Confraternity will function to the same degree as the Director.

Appointment of the Local Director.

This is reserved to the Master of the Order or the Prior Provincial of any Province of the Dominican Order, with the exceptions listed below:

- In the Dominican churches and chapels, the Superior at the time is *ipso facto* the Director.
- In churches or chapels which are in the care of the Diocesan Clergy, the Master of the Order or Prior Provincial appoints the Director with the consent of the Local Ordinary. Here again the appointment must be of one who holds an office with the Church, usually, the Pastor, or the equivalent, and his successors delegated through the office of the Provincial Director.

The Duties of the Local Director.

The primary duty of the Local Director is to enroll members in the Confraternity and to see to the spiritual welfare of its members. The Director is tasked with supporting the Confraternity and building unity among its members. To this end and within the framework listed above, the Local Director has all the necessary authority and power to develop and build his Confraternity in accordance with the needs and conditions of the local community. The administration of the Confraternity has been wisely restricted to broad spiritual principles and to the bare necessities of the organization, so that the Local Director and Confraternity will be left free to guide as local circumstances demand. So much depends upon the good use of the enthusiasm of the members by the Director, who can easily channel it into great apostolic activities.

It is also the solemn responsibility of the Local Director to keep and safeguard the Official Register of the Confraternity. The Official Register should be kept with the Sacramental Records of the parish or chapel.

Traditionally, the Local Director also has the power to:

- To bless candles and roses if needed by the local Confraternity.
- Diligently take care to have the Rosary publicly recited at the altar of the Confraternity (if it exists) daily, or as frequently as possible, especially on the feasts of the Blessed Virgin.
- Preside or delegate administration the pious exercises of the Confraternity. One of the primary expressions of the Confraternity is a Solemn Procession in honor of the Blessed Mary, Mother of God, which can place on the first Sunday of each month, and especially appropriate on the first Sunday of October.

Special Organization of the Confraternity

The provisions of the official Constitution of the Rosary Altar Society make it possible to adopt and use the Rosary Confraternity to fit the particular needs and circumstances of the locality in which it is established. A great deal of good can be accomplished by the use of such means. There is no need of making the Confraternity any more than a spiritual association as it is simply outlined in the Constitution *Ubi Primum.* Perhaps in many places it will function better left simply as such. In other situations, where it can utilize the apostolic spirit of the members, it can be an instrument of great good.

In drawing up additional rules or constitutions for the Confraternity two points must be kept in mind:

- Nothing can be removed from the laws of the Confraternity, especially in regard to the gratuitous inscription of members.
- The statutes must be approved by the local Bishop, and they have no binding force and power without his approval.

As to the nature of these Constitutions, they may vary from the very detailed Constitutions which have been suggested in the past to a very simple and loose association. Practice and experience indicate that these following points should be kept in mind when forming a Rosary Association:

- Any other work which might be adopted should not overshadow the primary responsibility of the members to pray and promote the Holy Rosary of our Blessed Mother. This can happen quite easily. The work of Confraternity must come first and always be the important concern of the organization, anything else is secondary.
- A rather simple method is to form a Rosary Committee out of those members of the Confraternity who are really

interested in propagating the Rosary and the Confraternity. Such a committee can function quite easily and be a close knit group who will carry on the essential work of the Confraternity.
- Another method which is practical is to use a parish organization already in existence to take over the work, or to set up a committee in the organization to perform the necessary functions.

7 The Establishment of the Confraternity

The Constitution *Ubi Primum,* other declarations of the Holy See, and Canon Law laid down the conditions and rules for the establishment of a Confraternity.

The Place of Establishment

The following are the regulations:

- "The Confraternity of the Rosary may be established in any church or public oratory to which the faithful have free access."
- The Confraternity may not be established in a semi-public or private oratory.
- Nor may a Confraternity be established "in the church of nuns and other pious women living in community," because it would place a restriction on who can be enrolled in that Confraternity. However, with special permission of the Local Ordinary it may be granted but for women only, to enable them to gain the indulgences and enjoy the privileges of the Confraternity. The Confraternity in that case may not function as an organization, but only inscribe names of women in the Register.
- "... More than one sodality of the Most Holy Rosary must not exist in one and the same place.... In large cities, as

has been already granted, there may be several sodalities of the Rosary; these for their lawful institution must be proposed by the Ordinary to the Master of the Order." Where the Confraternity is already in existence, special permission from the Local Ordinary must be obtained for the establishment of another.

Petition for the Establishment of a Confraternity

Ordinarily the petition for the establishment of a new Confraternity is handled through the Provincial Director. (The address is given above.) The Provincial Director obtains the Document of Establishment from the Master of the Order or Prior Provincial, who alone have the power to establish a new Confraternity.

> Written permission (and this is necessary for validity) must be obtained from the Local Ordinary. The Vicar General of a diocese ordinarily does not have the authority to give this permission, unless it has been specially delegated, which must be stated in the permission. (Forms for this Episcopal permission may be obtained from the Provincial Director.)
>
> The petition for the establishment of a new Confraternity must, besides having the written permission of the Local Ordinary, state the name of the city, church and diocese, where the Confraternity is to be established and who is to have the office of Director.

The Transferal of the Confraternity

Once a Confraternity is canonically established, it endures in *perpetuum.* Even, if it should cease to function for more or less a long period, it retains its rights and privileges and it may be restored to its former state without a new act of establishment.

The following are the rules on the transferal of a Confraternity:

- If a new church is built to replace an old or destroyed one, and is substantially in the same location and under the same title, the Confraternity is transferred to the new church with all its rights and privileges.
- In any other case a new Document of Establishment must be obtained.

In Cases of Doubtful Establishment of the Confraternity

The following are the rules for cases where it is questionable as to whether or not a Confraternity has been validly established:

- If the Document of Establishment has been issued and its execution is doubtful, it suffices to supply the omission, publicly or privately, in the presence of at least two witnesses, by repeating the act of establishment and renewing the inscription of names in the Register if any have been made.
- If it is doubtful whether a Document was issued, i.e., it is lost and there is not certain proof of its issuance, a new Document should be requested and the establishment is to be made as if no Confraternity had existed. The inscription of names in the Register must be renewed. Presumption and good faith are not sufficient for canonical establishment.
- If there is positive indication that the Confraternity has been established, in the absence of the Document, the Confraternity is to be taken as validly established.

8 Sample By-Laws of the Rosary Altar Society

NOTE: These By-Laws are proposed as a tentative program for the Rosary Societies and may be altered at the discretion of the Local Director/Rector.

CONCERNING THE NAME OF THE SOCIETY

I

The Rosary Society is understood to be the Society of the Rosary Altar, an integral phase of the Most Holy Rosary Confraternity whose norm are identified with the Church of *Santa Maria sopra Minerva* at Rome, Italy. (This part of the proposed bylaws is where the Individual Confraternity chooses its name. In this example "Rosary Society" is being used. Other examples could be Holy Rosary Society, Rosary Altar Society, or Society of the Rosary Altar to name a few.)

II

When the charter of the Prior Provincial or Master of the Order of the Dominicans and the consent of the Ordinary of this church (chapel) have been received before the prescribed Ceremony of establishment, we declare the Rosary Altar Society of this church to have been canonically established with all the rights and privileges of the Confraternity of the Most Holy Rosary. The title or name of the group, for example "The Society of the Rosary Altar," signifies that this society of the Rosary Confraternity is a moral person in the sense of the Code of Canon Law. Likewise, the Rosary Altar designated in the Ceremony of canonical establishment is the shrine center of this society.

CONCERNING THE LOCAL DIRECTOR / RECTOR
III

The Local Director or Rector of the Rosary Altar Society is the pastor, (chaplain) of the church (chapel) and his successors. The document *Instrumentum peractae erectionis* is an authentication of the Rector's rights. A copy of this document shall be kept affixed inside the register of the society and a duplicate of the same document shall be forwarded at the time of canonical establishment to the archives of the Master of the Order of the Dominicans. The canonical successor, with the equivalent jurisdiction of the original Rector named in the aforesaid document, automatically enjoys all the authority, the rights and privileges of a Rector of the Rosary Society.

IV

Assistant priests may be delegated by the aforesaid Rector or Local Director to assist in the work of the Society.

V

The rights and faculties of the Rector or Local director of the Rosary Society or of his assistant priest are official rather than personal. However, all the faithful, even those not parishioners, are eligible to be received into membership either in person or by written request.

VI

The Rector or Local Director of the Society of the Rosary is the true source of authority for the administration of the activities of the members. The may, at his discretion, decree the election of any official or dispense with the same.

CONCERNING OFFICERS

VII

In the administration of the Rosary Altar Society the officers shall include: the chaplain or spiritual director; the president; the vice-president; the secretary; and the treasurer. (These officers should be dictated by the needs of the Society. Remember, a Confraternity or Society may be rather small and not need this many officers.)

VIII

The time for the election of officers, the duration of an officer's term and the duties of each shall be determined by the Rector or by the Officers and the Spiritual Director.

CONCERNING MEMBERSHIP

IX

In the United States the officers and regular membership for public activities, etc., in the church shall be open to Catholic men and women. Children whose names will have been enrolled are considered to be participants in the strictly spiritual benefits. The Rector, however, has full discretion regarding the age of the membership.

X

All the living faithful of the Catholic church who have reached the age of reason and are able to recite the full twenty decades of the Marian Rosary once a week may be enrolled as members of the Rosary Confraternity within the Rosary Society.

CONCERNING MEETINGS

XI

The Rosary Altar Society of the Rosary Confraternity shall hold its regular meetings once a month, at a time and place determined by the officers with the approval of the Rector.

XII

The first Sunday of the month can be designated as Rosary Sunday. It was the customary day for the corporate reception of Holy Communion. However, any day of the week may now be selected for Corporate Communion. Note: Corporate Communion refers to a scheduled Mass attended by the members of the Confraternity.

XIII

A Rosary procession, to which a plenary indulgence is attached, may be solemnly held in the church on the first Sunday of each month—or on some other Sunday at the discretion of the Rector. The first Sunday of October, the month of the Rosary, should be solemnized by special ceremonies.

XIV

The public recitation of the Rosary shall be held especially during the month of October.

XV

Special assessments for charitable or sanctuary activities may be voted at the regular meetings of the Rosary Society.

XVI

A publicly announced Mass shall be offered for each deceased member of the Altar Rosary Society.

XVII

Five decades of the Holy Rosary shall be recited during the Rosarian's visit beside the remains of each deceased member before the day of the funeral Mass. A plenary indulgence may be gained for this spiritual exercise if it is performed by a group of Rosarians. (Cf. *Enchiridion on Indulgences,* 1969, No. 48.)

XVIII

The Rosary Society By-Laws can be added to or amended according to local circumstances.

PART II

ROSARIAN RITUAL AND FORMULARY

1 Manner of Establishing the Confraternity of the Holy Rosary

The priest delegated by the Most Reverend Master of the Order or Prior Provincial should diligently follow the conditions expressed in the letter granting faculties.

At a suitable time, he should proceed to the altar designated for the Confraternity (or the main altar) and there intone or recite the hymn *Veni Creator* (Come Creator Spirit).

When the hymn is completed by the choir, he enters the pulpit and preaches a sermon on the excellence of the Rosary devotion and explains the benefits of Confraternity membership.

When the sermon is finished, certain hymns in honor of the Queen of the Rosary may be sung.

The delegated priest, having returned to the altar, puts on a white stole and turning towards the people makes the following declaration in a loud voice:

> I Father <u>NN</u> of the Order of Preachers (or <u>NN</u> a priest) in the name of the Most Reverend Father <u>NN</u> Master of the Order of Preachers, and by the authority delegated to me by him, institute and establish the Confraternity of the Most Holy Rosary of the Virgin Mary, the Mother of God, in this Church of <u>St. N.</u> and I declare it instituted

and established with all the graces, privileges and indulgences granted and to be granted by the Holy See to the Confraternities of the Most Holy Rosary.

The establishment of the Confraternity consists in the above declaration. For validity this act is required.

After this the priest says:

> Likewise, I declare that the Reverend Rector of this Church of <u>St. N.</u>, and his successor in this office in perpetuity, is nominated and instituted as Rector of this Confraternity now established with all the rights and faculties proper to this office by the aforesaid Most Reverend Master of the Order.

Next (if applicable) indicating the altar or chapel if of the Confraternity, he says:

> Likewise, I declare that this Altar (or this Chapel) of <u>St. N.</u> is set aside for the Confraternity, in order that the faithful may gain the indulgences there which have been granted by the Holy See to those who visit the chapel or altar of the Confraternity. In the name of the Father and of the Son and of the Holy Spirit. Amen.

(a) Only the priest named as delegate of the Prior Provincial or Master of the Order in the Document of Establishment can set up the Confraternity. If he is impeded, a substitute accepted by the Local Ordinary may do it.

(b) The formal act of establishment consists in the public declaration of the delegate in the presence of at least two witnesses, that the Confraternity is established according to the formula given in the Ceremony. This act is necessary for validity. It may be done privately, before two witnesses for a just cause, *e.g.,* reactivation of a Confraternity which has been inactive for many years.

(c) Notification of these activities should be signed by all those indicated and returned to the Provincial Director.

2 Solemn Reception Ceremony for Rosary Society Members

If the parish or chapel has a Rosary Altar it should be decorated with flowers and lighted candles. The priest vested in surplice and white stole, or if a religious priest the full habit with stole, leads the congregation in the recitation of five decades of the Rosary. The congregation then sings the *Veni Creator* or "Come Holy Ghost." The singing is followed by a sermon on Our Lady of the Rosary during which the priest explains briefly the privileges and duties of Rosarians.

I. Then the candidates to be received come forward and kneel, is possible each holding a candle and beads. The priest says to the group:

Priest: Do you wish to become members of the Confraternity of the Most Holy Rosary?
    Candidates: We do.
Priest: Do you promise to promote in every way possible the honor of Our Blessed Lady and devotion to her Rosary?
    Candidates: We do.
Priest: May God who has inspired you with these intentions grant you through the intercession of the Queen of the Most Holy Rosary grace to persevere.

II. The priest then begins the following prayer:

Priest : Our help is in the name of the Lord.
    R/ : Who made heaven and earth.
Priest: The Lord be with you.
    R/ : And with your spirit.

LET US PRAY
Almighty and Eternal God, Who by the death of Your Only Begotten Son, has restored this corrupted world that we might be free from eternal death and be led into the happiness of the kingdom of heaven; we beg You to look upon these Your servants, who desire to be enrolled among the children of the Society of the Most Holy Rosary of the Blessed Virgin, and through the merits of the Mother of God pour forth on these Your blessing so that those blessed may so live in this world that they might merit to be forever established among the sheep on Your right hand. Through Christ Our Lord, Amen.

III. Blessing of Rosaries *(see Formulary)*

IV. Blessing of Candles of the Rosary Altar Society *(see Formulary)*

V. Blessing of Rosary medal or pin *(see Formulary)*

    Optional: Blessing and distribution of natural roses to be taken home *(see Formulary)*.

VI. Admission into the Rosary Altar Society

> By the authority which I exercise and which is conceded to me by the Most Reverend Father Master of the Order of Preachers, I admit you to the Rosary Society, canonically called the Confraternity of the Most Holy Rosary, and I make you sharers in all the spiritual goods of the whole sacred Order of Preachers as well as the spiritual goods and works done through God's

grace throughout the world by all of the members of the Society of the Most Holy Rosary. In the name of the Father and of the Son and of the Holy Spirit. Amen.

VII. Then the members are blessed with holy water, each holding in the left hand a blessed Rosary candle and a pair of Rosary beads in the right hand, the priest goes to each one and says:
> Receive the sign of the living God, so called by the Most Holy Virgin herself; may it be to you a pledge of eternal life and a means to the attainment thereof. Amen.

(If a Rosary medal or pin is presented at this time, the priest says:)
> Receive this medal of the Society of the Most Holy Rosary and let it be for you a sign of your loyalty. Amen.

VIII. The priest says:
> Our help is in the name of the Lord.
> > R/. Who made heaven and earth.
> Priest: The Lord be with you.
> > R/. And with your spirit.

Priest : May all mighty God bless you, ☩ the Father, the Son, and the Holy Spirit. (A more solemn form of blessing may be substituted.)

3 Installation of Officers

The success of the Rosary Society depends to a great extent upon how well the officers perform their respective duties. To emphasize this fact, it is fitting that they be formally installed in their new posts. The following Installation Ceremony (or one similar to it) may be used for this purpose.

Installation Ceremony

This ceremony may be conducted in the church. The four officers, President, Vice-President, Secretary and Treasurer leave the pew and take their places (four prie-dieux may be arranged for them in the Sanctuary). The Spiritual Director or Pastor may make a brief address thanking the previous administration and congratulating the new officers about to be installed.

The <u>Spiritual Director</u> then says to the first officer:
> <u>Name</u>, our Rosary Society has by its election entrusted you with the office of President. Do you accept this office?"

<u>Officer</u>: I do accept.
<u>Spiritual Director</u>: Do you understand the duties of this office?
<u>Officer</u>: I do understand these duties.
<u>Spiritual Director</u>: Do you promise to fulfill all these duties conscientiously and to the best of your ability so that this Society may prosper and through it the Holy Rosary of Mary may be loved and honored?
<u>Officer</u>: For the greater honor and glory of Mary, Virgin of the Rosary, I do promise to fulfill all the duties of my office to the best of my ability.
<u>Spiritual Director</u>: I hereby declare you to be the President of the Rosary Society of <u>St. N.</u> Church and surrender to you the insignia of this office. May Our Divine Lord and His Blessed Mother, the Virgin of the Rosary, bless and prosper your efforts in our holy cause.

This formula is repeated for each officer. After the installation, the Spiritual Director may make a plea for the cooperation of the members.

PART III

ROSARY FORMULARY AND BLESSINGS FOR DIRECTORS OF SOCIETIES OF THE ROSARY

All of the following blessings can begin with following:

Presider: Our help is in the name of the Lord.
    R/: Who made heaven and earth.
Presider: The Lord be with you.
    R/: And with your spirit.
Presider: Let us pray…

1 Blessing of Rosaries

Almighty and merciful God, on account of Your very great love for us, You willed that Your only Begotten Son, Our Lord Jesus Christ, should come down from heaven to earth, and at the angel's message take flesh in the most sacred womb of Our Lady, the Most Blessed Virgin Mary, submit to death on the cross, and then rise gloriously from the dead on the third day, in order to deliver us from Satan's tyranny. We humbly beg You, in Your boundless goodness to bless ill and to sanctify ill these rosaries, which Your faithful Church has consecrated to the honor and praise of the Mother of Your Son. Let them be endowed with such power of the Holy Spirit, that who- ever carries one with them, or reverently keeps one in their home, or devoutly prays to You while meditating on the divine mysteries, according to the rules of this holy society, may fully share in all the graces, privileges, and indulgences which the Holy See has granted to this society. May they always and everywhere in this life be shielded from all enemies, visible and invisible, and at their death deserve to be presented to You by the Most Blessed Virgin Mary herself, Mother of God. Through the same Lord Jesus Christ, Your Son, who lives and reigns with You in the unity of the Holy Spirit, God for ever and ever.

R/. Amen

[They are sprinkled with holy water.]

Short Formula for Blessing of Rosaries

To the honor and glory of Mary, the Virgin Mother of God, in memory of the mysteries of the life, death and resurrection of Our Lord, the same Jesus Christ, may this crown of the Most Holy Rosary be blessed ✞ and sanctified ✞ in the name of the Father, ✞ and of the Son, and of the Holy Spirit. R/. Amen.

2 Blessing of Roses

God, You are the creator and upholder of the human race, the author of grace and the generous giver of eternal salvation, with Your holy blessings ✞ bless these roses which we beg You to bless, and which we offer this day in thanksgiving to You and in devotion and veneration towards the ever Blessed Virgin Mary of the Rosary. By the power of the holy cross pour out a heavenly ✞ blessing on these roses, which You have given to us to enjoy their pleasing fragrance and to alleviate sickness. By the sign of the holy ✞ cross let them be endowed with such blessing that the sick to whom they are brought, or who bring them to their homes, may be healed of their infirmities. May the devils depart, may they flee panic-stricken with their followers from these dwellings, nor may they any more dare to trouble those who serve You. Through Christ Our Lord.

R/. Amen.
[They are sprinkled with holy water.]

3 Blessing of Candles

Lord Jesus Christ, the true light that enlightens all who come into the world, by the prayers of the Blessed Virgin Mary, Your Mother, and the fifteen mysteries of her Rosary, pour out Your blessing ✝ on these candles and tapers, and sanctify ✝ them by the light of Your grace. Mercifully grant, that as these lights with their visible fire dispel the darkness of the night, so may the Holy Spirit with his invisible fire and splendor dispel the darkness of our vices. May He help us ever to discern, with the pure eye of the spirit, the things that are pleasing to You and of benefit to us, so that, in spite of the darkness and pitfalls of this world, we may come at last to the light that never fails. For You live and reign forever and ever.

R/. Amen.

[They are sprinkled with holy water.]

4 Blessing of Rosary Medals or Pins

GOD, by whose word all things are made holy, pour down Your blessings ✝ on these medals (pins) which You created. Grant that whoever giving thanks to You, uses them in accordance with Your law and Your will, may, by calling on Your Holy Name, receive through Your aid, health of body and protection of soul, through Christ Our Lord.

R/. Amen.

PART IV

ROSARIAN CUSTOMS AND DEVOTIONS

1 The Monthly Rosary Procession

The monthly Rosary procession is a longstanding tradition within the Confraternity. The following is some background information and guidelines:

1. "Among the pious exercises of the Confraternity the first place is, with reason, given to the solemn procession in honor of the Mother of God, which takes place on the first Sunday of each month and especially on the first Sunday of October. St. Pius V commended this ancient custom; Gregory XIII mentions it among the 'praiseworthy exercises and customs of the Confraternity, "and many Sovereign Pontiffs have attached to it special indulgences."

2. The permission of the Local Ordinary is not necessary for the Rosary Confraternity enjoys the right to have such processions without any previous permission. The Local Ordinary has the right only, if he wishes, to prescribe the route which the procession is to use.

3. "In order that the ceremony may never be omitted, at least within the church when it is impossible to have it in the open air, we extend to all the Directors of the Confraternity the privilege granted by Benedict XIII to the Order of Preachers, of transferring the procession to another Sunday, when, for any reason, it can- not take place on the first Sunday of the month."

4. "But when, on account of lack of space and number of the faithful, the solemn procession cannot conveniently take place in the church, we permit that while the priest with his attendants make the circuit of the church, the members of the Confraternity who are present may gain all the indulgences attached to the procession."

5. The ceremonies for the procession are left greatly to the choice of the Local Director. It is recommended that the Litany of the Blessed Virgin be sung or when this is not possible, it may be recited. Recitation of the Rosary is also an integral part of the procession. The procession concludes with the Litany. As long as the Litany is said, other fitting hymns, prayers, etc., may be used at the discretion of the Director.

2 Rosary Candles and Roses

The candle and the rose have long been connected with the Rosary beads in the history of the Rosary devotion. The Dominican faculties possessed by Rectors of the Rosary Confraternity include the blessings of Rosary candles and roses. Roses are usually blessed and distributed on the first Sunday of October, or on the feast of the Blessed Virgin of the Rosary on October 7, but they may be blessed on any festival of the Rosary Society.

The history of blessed roses records many cures and favors through the touching of the sick and infirm with blessed rose petals. Blessed candles are prescribed for the solemn reception of new members of the Rosary Society. They can also be carried in the Rosary procession held on the first Sunday of each month.

3 The Fifteen Saturdays of the Rosary

This devotion consists in receiving Holy Communion on fifteen consecutive Saturdays (or Sundays) in commemoration of the original fifteen mysteries of the Rosary. Its intention is honoring Jesus and Mary, and of obtaining through Mary's intercession the grace of a happy death as well as other special intentions for which we ask. With this devotion one should also pray for the Pope's intentions, the propagation of the faith, and for the souls in purgatory.

In order that this devotion may be fruitful, all who practice it should try to imitate the virtues of Jesus and Mary by constant and devout meditation on their most holy lives. Hence, on each Saturday it will be necessary to recite and meditate on five Mysteries of the Rosary.

This devotion of fifteen Saturdays can be practiced at any time during the year, either with the intention of obtaining some special favor, or as an act of thanksgiving, or from devotion, and when ended may be started again immediately. The devotion of the fifteen Saturdays is often made as a preparation for the feast of the Blessed Virgin of the Rosary, which falls on October 7. If the external solemnity of the feast be celebrated on the first Sunday of October the indulgence may be gained on that day.

4 Rosary for the Dead

It is customary for a committee of Rosarians to visit the place where the body of a deceased member reposes between the time of death and funeral, and to offer five decades of the Rosary for the soul of the beloved member. The five Glorious Mysteries are customarily recited.

At the conclusion of the Rosary the following prayers should be added:

Rosary Leader:

O God, Creator and Redeemer of all the faithful grant to the souls of your servants and handmaids the remission of all their sins that they may obtain by our loving prayers, the forgiveness which they have always desired. Who live and reign forever and ever.

R/: Amen

Leader: Eternal rest grant unto him (her), O Lord,

R/: And let perpetual light shine upon her (him).

All: May his (her) soul and the souls of all the faithful departed through the mercy of God rest in peace. Amen."

5 The Family Rosary

Pope Pius XI, in his Rosary encyclical *Ingravescentibus Malis* dated September 29, 1937, wrote on the blessings of the Family Rosary:

> "No Catholic custom is better suited to heal family troubles, to unite quarrelling partners, to instill love and obedience in the souls of children, to invoke health for the sick, to obtain rest for the souls in purgatory, than the recitation of the daily Rosary in the intimacy of the family circle." Members of a family who recite five decades of the Rosary together may gain a Plenary Indulgence. (Cf. *Enchiridion on Indulgences*, 1969, n. 48)

6 The Promises of Our Lady, Queen of the Rosary Given to Blessed Alan De Rupe, O.P. – Founder of the Confraternity

- Whoever will faithfully serve me by the recitation of the Rosary shall receive extraordinary graces.

- To all who recite my Rosary devoutly, I promise my special protection and very great graces.

- The Rosary will be a very powerful armor against hell. It will destroy vice, deliver from sin, and dispel heresy.

- The Rosary will make virtue and good works flourish and will obtain for souls the most abundant divine mercies; it will substitute in hearts love of God for love of the world, and elevate them to desire heavenly and eternal goods. Oh, that souls would sanctify themselves by this means!

- Those who trust themselves to me through the Rosary will not perish.

- Those who shall recite my Rosary piously, considering its Mysteries, will not be overwhelmed by misfortune, nor die a bad death. The sinner will be converted, the just will grow in grace and become worthy of eternal life.

- Whoever will have a true devotion for the Rosary shall not die without the Sacraments.

- Those who faithfully recite the Rosary shall have during their life and at their death the light of God, and the plenitude of His graces; at the moment of death they shall participate in the merits of the saints in heaven.

- I will deliver very promptly from purgatory the souls devoted to my Rosary.

- The true children of my Rosary will enjoy great glory in heaven.

- What you shall ask through the Rosary you shall obtain.

- Those who propagate my Rosary will obtain through me aid in all their necessities.

- I have obtained from my Son that all the members of the Rosary Confraternity shall have the saints of heaven for their intercessors in life and death.

- Those who recite my Rosary faithfully are all my beloved children, the brothers and sisters of Jesus Christ.

- Devotion to my Rosary is a special sign of God's loving plan for our salvation.

7 Rosary Novenas

The Rosary Novena is suggested for the use of the faithful in conformity with the wishes of many of the Sovereign Pontiffs who have recommended the efficacy of Mary's Rosary not only for private use but also for public devotions in the church. There are three traditional forms of the Rosary Novena.

I

The first form of the Rosary Novena consists of nine consecutive days of public or private Rosary devotions in accordance with the example of Our Lady and the Apostles who remained together in prayer from the Ascension of Our Lord until Pentecost Sunday when the Holy Spirit, the Third Person of the Blessed Trinity descended upon them.

II

The salutary custom of making six consecutive novenas of Rosary devotion originated at the famous shrine of Our Lady of the Rosary at Pompeii, Italy. The devotion consists of three successive novenas of petition, or request for a special favor, followed by three successive novenas of thanksgiving for all the graces of God even if the special favor has not been granted.

III

The third form of Rosary Novena is called the Perpetual Novena or the Novena of Weeks. It consists in attending public Rosary services in a church on one designated day of the week.

Order of Exercises of the Rosary Novena

Opening Novena Prayers

These are the Opening Prayers to be said before the recitation of the Rosary on each day of the novena:

Open my mouth, O Lord, to bless Your Holy Name; cleanse my heart from all vain and unholy thoughts; inspire my mind and inflame my will, that I may worthily, attentively and devoutly recite Mary's Rosary as a Psalter of homage to You, and in my Rosary prayer, may I merit to be heard in the presence of Your Majesty, through Christ Our Lord. Amen.

O Lord, in union with that divine intention with which You praised and accomplished the Divine Will while on earth, I offer this recitation of the Most Holy Rosary for the wants of Our Holy Mother the Church, for all heretics, all sinners, all those severely tempted, for all the sick and dying and for the suffering souls in purgatory.

O Lord, grant me the grace of a good confession, which I will make as soon as possible, to insure my union with You and Your Immaculate Mother Mary during this Rosary Novena. Amen.

The Rosary is then Prayed in Normal Dominican Fashion

Special attention is to be paid to the petitions to Our Lady for each mystery listed below.

Novena Prayers: Act of Consecration to the Queen of the Rosary

O, Mary, my Mother, Queen of the Most Holy Rosary, I dedicate myself entirely to you, and as proof of my devotion, I consecrate to you this day, the faculties of my mind, the senses of my body, my heart, my soul, my entire being. Preserve and protect me always as your loving possession. O Queen of the Holy Rosary, Mother of God and my Mother, you who have great power in heaven, who never refuse the prayers of your loving children who trust in you, obtain for me the favors so near my heart. I ask them through your Most Holy Rosary, our beautiful heritage, given to Dominicans for the help and consolation of your loving children. O Blessed Mother with your Rosary in my hands, I place my petition in your care.

8 The Dominican Way of Praying the Rosary

The Order of Friars Preachers has traditionally begun the Rosary in a way that differs from the most common form. It is based on a more ancient form of praying the Rosary in an antiphonal choir (prayer) setting. It begins with the verses and responses that begin the Liturgy of the Hours and the Angelic Salutation which is the first part of the Hail Mary. The Dominican way of praying the Rosary is as follows (Note: Because this ancient form of the Rosary predates the revelations of Our Lady at Fatima, the Fatima prayers are usually not added after the doxology "Glory be…"):

V: In the Name of the Father, and of the Son, and of the Holy Spirit.
    R/: Amen

V: Hail, Mary, full of grace, the Lord is with Thee
    R/: Blessed art Thou among women, and blessed is the fruit of Thy womb, Jesus.

V: Lord, open my lips
    R/: And my mouth will proclaim Your praise.

V: God, come to my assistance
    R/: Lord, make haste to help me.

V: Glory be to the Father, and to the Son and to the Holy Spirit.
    R/: As it was in the beginning, is now, and ever shall be, world without end. Amen. (Alleluia!)

V: [Announce the first mystery for the day prescribed by local custom. Pray the five decades of the Mystery. Of course each decade starts with the "Our Father," then 10 "Hail Marys" and ends with doxology "Glory be…"]

Note: The Dominican way of reciting the Rosary in a group also differs from common ways of praying the Rosary. The leader and the assembly alternate who begins the "Our Father" and "Hail Mary." After the leader announces the Mystery, she or he will begin the "Our Father" prayer and "Hail Mary" prayers for the first, third, and fifth mystery. The assembly begins the prayers for the second and fourth mystery. While it is preferred that Rosarians pray the Holy Rosary in this manner it is not required. If local custom or the comfort level of the local Society dictates, using a more the common form of the Rosary is acceptable.

The Joyful Mysteries

First- **The Annunciation** - Ask for Mary's humility.
Second- **The Visitation** - Ask for Mary's spirit of fraternal charity.
Third- **The Nativity** - Ask to become poor in spirit.
Fourth- **The Presentation** - Ask for Mary's purity.
Fifth- **The Finding of Christ in the Temple** - Ask for Mary's love of Jesus.

The Sorrowful Mysteries

First- **The Agony in the Garden** - Ask for Mary's resignation.
Second- **The Scourging at the Pillar** - Ask for the spirit of mortification.
Third- **The Crowning with Thorns** - Ask for Mary's meekness.
Fourth –**The Carrying of the Cross** - Ask for Mary's patience in suffering.
Fifth –**The Crucifixion** - Ask for Mary's love of God.

The Luminous Mysteries

First- **Christ's Baptism in the Jordan** - Ask Mary's help to live out your Baptismal promises.
Second- **The Wedding Feast at Cana** - Ask Mary to intercede for married people.
Third- **The Proclamation of the Kingdom** - Ask for Mary's understanding of God's word.
Fourth- **The Transfiguration** - Ask for Mary's understanding of Jesus, her Son.
Fifth- **The Institution of the Eucharist** - Ask for Mary's help to live life in the Sacraments.

The Glorious Mysteries

First- **The Resurrection** - Ask for Mary's lively faith.
Second- **The Ascension** - Ask for Mary's firm hope.
Third- **The Descent of the Holy Spirit** - Ask for Mary's zeal.
Fourth –**The Assumption** - Ask for Mary's loyalty.
Fifth- **The Coronation of Mary Queen of Heaven** - Ask Mary to intercede for the gift of final perseverance.

Concluding Prayers of the Five Decades.

All: Hail, Holy Queen, Mother of Mercy, our life, our sweetness and our hope! To you do we cry, poor banished children of Eve; to you we send up our sighs, mourning and weeping in this vale of tears. Turn, then, most gracious advocate, your eyes of mercy toward us, and after this our exile, show unto us the blessed fruit of your womb, Jesus. O clement, O loving, O sweet Virgin Mary.

V: Queen of the Most Holy Rosary, pray for us.
R/: That we may be made worthy of the promises of Christ.

V: Let us pray.

All: O God, whose only begotten Son, by His life, death and resurrection, has purchased for us the rewards of eternal life, grant, we beseech Thee, that meditating upon these mysteries of the Most Holy Rosary of the Blessed Virgin Mary, we may imitate what they contain and obtain what they promise, through the same Christ, Our Lord. *Amen.*

V: May the Divine assistance remain with us always.
    R/: Amen.
V: May the souls of the Faithful departed, through the mercy of God, rest in peace.
    R/: Amen.

9 Optional Rosary Prayers

Prayer After the Joyful Mysteries

O, Queen of the Most Holy Rosary help me to translate into my life the virtues so beautifully exemplified by you in the Joyful Mysteries. By your love of purity at the *Annunciation* whereby you accepted the divine maternity while preserving your vow of virginity, preserve me from the contagion of sin. By your charity at the *Visitation* whereby joy was brought to the household of your cousin, Elizabeth, help me to show charity to my neighbor. By the virtue of poverty that prevailed at the *Nativity,* teach me to have tender love for God's poor. By the spirit of obedience to the law of God at the *Presentation* in the Temple, assist me always to be a faithful child of our holy Mother, the Church. By your joy in the *Finding of Jesus* among the doctors in the Temple, help me ever to seek true happiness in the Blessed Sacrament where Christ dwells among us. *Amen.*

Prayer After the Sorrowful Mysteries

Keep me, O Blessed Mother, in conformity with the Divine Will as was your Son during the *Agony in the Garden*, when He said, "Not My Will but Yours be done." When sin calls me away from God, may I be mindful of the *Scourging*. Against the spirit of pride impress deeply upon me the memory of my Savior and His *Thorn-Crowned Head*. When my feet are about to stray from the paths of virtue remind me of the *Carrying of the Cross*. Let me never forget the *Crucifixion* when the dying Christ forgave His enemies, promised Paradise to a thief and gave You to me as my Mother. Amen

Prayer After the Luminous Mysteries

Holy Mary Mother of God, I ask your prayers for the grace to truly live life in the Sacraments. The light your Son brought to the world shines most brightly in the Sacraments He instituted for His Holy Church. Allow me to live my Baptismal promises to the fullest, experience the healing He brought to the sick, and be confirmed in the strength of the Holy Spirit. Allow me to serve others with the same love your Son showed as I strive to live my vocation, whether it be to marriage, religious life, or the chaste single life of service. Strengthen me in my love for His most Holy Body and Blood, to better preach and bring The Luminous Word, Our Lord Jesus Christ to all the nations as you have done my Holy Mother! Amen.

Prayer After the Glorious Mysteries

Give me, O Queen of the Most Holy Rosary, the courage and confidence that comes through the *Resurrection*. Help me always to look forward to the fulfillment of the great hope inspired by the *Ascension*. Teach me to live in the spirit of the first Novena which you and the Apostles made in preparation for the *Coming of the Holy Spirit*. Inspire me with the glory of your *Assumption* and the joy that was yours when at your

Coronation you were made Queen of Heaven and Earth. Amen.

10 Prayer for the Rosary Apostolate of the Confraternity

O good Jesus, if sinners only knew You, they would never offend You! Listen to the prayer of my heart and soul, that I may become a generous and loving apostle of the Most Holy Rosary. Let my every breath pour forth the eloquence of the five Joyful Mysteries. Like the love and devotion Your mother had for You, grant me true wisdom and understanding of Your life and teaching as poured forth in the Luminous Mysteries. With a love far exceeding the tenderness of a mother's love, let me through the five Sorrowful Mysteries assist and console the most abject of sinners. And with the help of Your grace and the protection of Mary, the Mother of God, and my own Mother, let me merit the reward of sorrow turned into joy and eternally contemplate the five Glorious Mysteries. Amen.

11 Rules on Indulgences

Indulgences in General

In 1967 Pope Paul issued his Apostolic Constitution on Indulgences, *Indulgentiarum Doctrina.* This document contains the current rules on indulgences, and reaffirms the power of the Church to grant indulgences to the faithful for the remission of temporal punishment due to sin. The 1983 Code of Canon Law (CCl n. 992-997) is based heavily on this document.

The focus of *Indulgentiarum Doctrina* was to clarify the Church's teaching on indulgences in order to correct abuses and misunderstands of the past and makes them more spiritually fruitful in the modern world. In order to highlight the importance of this ancient practice, the Pope greatly reduced the number of circumstances under which indulgences could be gained. He also shifted the focus from the external act of gaining the indulgence, for example from objects or places, to the internal disposition of the person seeking its spiritual benefits.

1. An indulgence is the cancellation in God's sight of the temporal punishment due for sin, when the sin's guilt has already been pardoned through the Sacrament of Reconciliation. With the Church as intermediary, a Christian who is properly disposed and who fulfills certain well defined conditions can obtain an indulgence.

2. An indulgence is partial if it frees a Christian partially from the temporal punishment due for his/her sins, plenary if it frees wholly.

3. Both partial and plenary indulgences can always be applied to the dead, but only by way of suffrage (through our prayers). An indulgence cannot be applied to a living person.

4. A partial indulgence is without any reference to time whether in days or years.

5. A plenary indulgence can be gained only once a day, except by those who stand on the threshold of death.

6. To gain a plenary indulgence the person concerned must perform the indulgenced act. Three conditions must also be satisfied several days before or after the indulgenced act. They are reception the Sacramental of Reconciliation, reception of Holy Eucharistic, and praying for the Pope's intentions.

In addition, the person concerned must be free from all attachment to sin, even to venial sin. If this complete integrity is not present or the above conditions are not fulfilled, the indulgence is only partial.

12 Indulgences Granted to the Members of the Rosary Confraternity

A plenary indulgence, under the usual conditions, is granted to all members:

1) On the day of enrollment.

2) On Christmas and Easter, and the Feast of the Annunciation, the Assumption, Our Lady of the Rosary, the Immaculate Conception, the Presentation of Jesus at the Temple.

A plenary indulgence may be gained (under the usual conditions) when the Rosary is said in church or public oratory, in a family, a religious community or pious association. Otherwise a partial indulgence is gained. A partial indulgence may be gained by those who pray the blessed Rosary.

APPENDIX: CONTACTS

Local Provincial Promoters of the Confraternity of the Holy Rosary

For the Central United States
http://opcentral.org/confraternity-of-the-holy-rosary

For the Western United States
http://www.rosary-center.org/

For the Eastern United States
http://rosaryconfraternity.org/
Confraternity of the Most Holy Rosary
Dominican Province of Saint Joseph
280 North Grant Avenue
Columbus, OH 43215
Phone: (614) 240-5929 Fax: (614) 240-5928

For the Southern United States
Promoter of Confraternity of the Holy Rosary
St. Anthony of Padua Church
4640 Canal St.
New Orleans, LA 70119

The International Rosary Website
http://rosarium.op.org

For Argentina
http://www.op.org.ar/rosario.php

For Australia, New Zealand, the Solomon Islands, and Papua New Guinea
http://rosary.op.org.au/

For India
Promoter of Holy Rosary
Dominic Ashram
near SFS College Seminary
Hill Nagpur, 440006
MAHARASHTRA, INDIA

For Ireland
http://www.rosarycentre.com/confraternity.htm

For the United Kingdom
http://english.op.org/Rosary.html

For Southern Africa
Promoter of the Holy Rosary
The General Vicariate of Southern Africa
St. Dominic's Catholic Parish
P.O. Box 198
87 Jan Hofmeyr Road
WELCOM 9460 South Africa

www.ingramcontent.com/pod-product-compliance
Lightning Source LLC
Chambersburg PA
CBHW061257040426
42444CB00010B/2408